I0004709

FROM IDEA TO ONLINE IN 24 HOURS

How To Quickly Get Your Website Online And Get Back To Working On Your Craft

CLIFF HUIZENGA

From Idea To Online In 24 Hours: How To Quickly Get
Your Website Online And Get Back To Working On Your Craft.

http://cliffpro.com

ISBN: 978-1511767897

TABLE OF CONTENTS

This book is dedicated to anyone who's looking for the push they need to get their project off the ground. Never put your dreams on hold. Start now.

For my wife, Jessica, who gives me the encouragement and support in everything I do. We do this together.

And for the Quonders group for the motivation to get off my ass and finally write my first book. Thanks for the push I needed, Scrivs and gang.

PREFACE

One morning in 2013, my wife, Jessica (the bestest ever[1]), woke up, almost popping up from a dream and tells me, "I want to open my own shop where I can sell confetti to people."

At the time, we had no idea how that would be possible.

We both went to college as our parents wanted, because it was "known" that higher education was the key to a well-paying job; What we got for our "education" were decent-paying jobs and around $100,000 in student loan debt. Wanting to pursue our dreams had to be put aside to pay the bills. Doing the same thing in and out every day gave a fine balance, but didn't feel rewarding.

So, we took a chance. We had no idea how to run an online shop and how to market confetti to the masses. But, between her creative vision and my technical skills, we

---

[1] Totally not written in by Jessica.

knew we had the ability to give it a try, even with our very limited resources.

Today, we both co-own the business, The Confetti Bar (theconfettibar.com), which she runs full-time from its new location on North Main St. in our home town. We've also just launched a reseller program, hoping to expand our business even further and will be attending trade shows to grow our business even more.

And how did it get from an idea and virtually no budget to a full-blown business? By getting our website online. And we did so in a very short amount of time.

This book was written to help you get your idea from a nearly-impossible dream and turn it into a reality. Follow this book and I'll walk you through setting up your first website, learning some of the technical bits you'll need to know and thinking about ideas for the future.

By the end of this book, and by the end of the day, your website should be online and ready to start building your plans toward success.

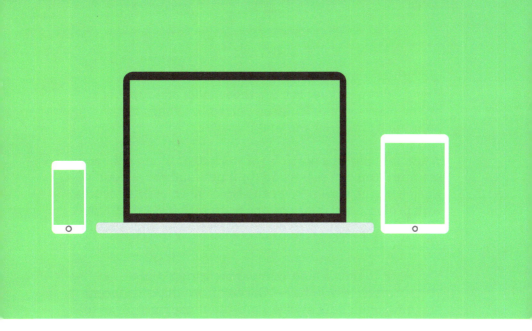

WHY HAVE AN ONLINE PRESENCE?

Let's start off with a straight-forward fact[2]: It is easier to start your business today than it ever has been in the history of man. Run outside your door, scream to the heavens, "I am open for business!" and you've started a business.

Of course, it takes a lot more work to actually run a business.

But now, with the Internet, you have more tools available to you than you ever had before. Most of which require very little technical skills to get started. Almost all of them have some sort of technical support for the things you can't control or don't understand.

[2] Opinion, but I promise it's true.

And that's awesome! Having these tools and support online leaves you to focus on perfecting your craft, building a presence and making sales.

You want to have a portfolio of work to go along with your resume? You can make one right now and share your work with the world! You can also have an online resume with professional connections to go with it via sites like LinkedIn. Connect with other professionals and land the job of your dreams!

You want to start a blog/online magazine about a specific passion you have? Choose from many different blogging platforms, stylize a pre-made theme and get to writing. Also, you can monetize your writings through advertisements and affiliate marketing, all with free resources to explain how to do so, like ProBlogger and CopyBlogger. You can build an audience that brings in enough revenue and quit your day job, creating your own dream job!

You want to take things you make at home and start selling them professionally? Start up an online shop and look like a big business, which in turn will get you sales like a big business. Gain customers, grow in size, form partnerships and hit it big!

Of course, if it's really that easy, why aren't more people doing these things? 3 reasons:

- **Actually, they are.** You might not think about it, but everyone has to start somewhere, right? They're the ones you see on the news or in your news feeds on your favorite social media sites who are creating and doing and growing. They run big name businesses, they're creating products you buy and they are changing the world.
- **Hard work is required.** Many people would rather not disrupt their normal routine than work hard to

pursue something that could change not only their life but the world around them.

- **People are their own worst enemy.** Along with hard work, some people just don't put their passions as their first priorities and, therefore, they never happen. Excuses come up like, "I don't have time" or "I don't know where to start."

That's where this guide comes in.

This is not a comprehensive guide on how to completely get something set up online (but, hey, if enough people read this book, maybe more guides will be created to accommodate those needs). What this book will do is get you online, initially ready to do what you need to with ease and get you over those excuse hurdles.

Living naturally, purposefully, and sugar free

w Veggie Rolls w/ Pot o' Gold Dipping Sauce

Food
Vanilla Bean Coconut Milk Whipped Cream

Food
Coconut Shortbread

Quick Case Study: Simple Unsweet

Simple Unsweet (simpleunsweet.com), a healthy recipe blog for those with special dietary needs, was another idea born from my wife. Along with The Confetti Bar, she has amazing vision for creative endeavors. But, with this one in particular, she didn't want the development of the site to take a few weeks, but in days or less.

In one day, we were able to:

- Purchased a domain name: simpleunsweet.com;
- Create a dedicated Gmail account for the site;
- Setup WordPress hosting with WP Engine;
- Pointed domain to hosting via DNS changes;
- Search and purchase a cheap theme for usage;
- Upload a custom logo quickly made in Photoshop;
- Create the interior pages of the site with content;
- Create dedicated Twitter, Facebook, Pinterest and Instagram accounts;
- Join Amazon Associates for affiliate marketing;
- Write 3 blog posts to give the site content; and
- Share the posts across social media channels.

We made it all happen in a few hours.

She turned a simple thought, an idea out of the blue, into a fully-functioning blog that went live the same day. It's still a pet project, but it's still growing in content, readership and has the potential to grow.

Of course, being of a more "geek mindset," I was able to help her get her vision up so quickly. Like my wife, you probably have a vague idea where to start looking, but don't know how to proceed, or started off but stopped when you hit a wall with technical issues.

This guide will help you do all the things mentioned above.

And we're going to do all of this today. Starting now.

SET YOUR GOALS

The Importance of Professional Image

It doesn't matter whether you're trying to set up an online portfolio to land a job, or if you want to start selling your awesome product to the masses; People see a huge difference in a person's professional image based on how they present themselves.

Domain Name vs. Freebie Service

If you were looking to hire someone for your job or buy a person's product, how would you react if they showed you their:

- own hosted design portfolio (their-name.com) vs. deviantart profile page;
- own blog with insights to the industry (their-name.com/blog) vs. their tumblr site;

- or, own online storefront (their-store.com) vs. some-username.etsy.com?

Custom Email Address vs. Free-mail Address

Let's take this a step further. Suppose that same person has a resume or business card with their email address listed. Which would you respond to more favorably:

their-name@their-business-name.com or their-name-and-business@gmail.com?

Implied Impressions

Knowing *nothing* else about the person, there's already plenty of information about them just by seeing how they handle their online presence in a professional environment. By using only free services, they've already communicated that they haven't thought much about their business strategies, nor their professional image.

Keep in mind, this doesn't mean the person in question does not care about their professional image; they may simply not know how to obtain things like a custom domain name, web hosting, or an email address to match.

Unfortunately, being professional isn't going to be free. Luckily for you, it doesn't have to be expensive. And, it doesn't have to be difficult.

Wants vs. Needs

Before you get into obtaining these professional items, you need to evaluate what is most important to have up front and what is not exactly needed right away. Because of the number of options available to you online, you may be overwhelmed with what experts online say you should have and do.

The problem is, if you wait until you have all the things you think you need to start off, you'll never launch your site and will have just created another barrier for yourself.

What You Want Can Wait

It's a tough decision, but for the sake of getting yourself set up faster, you might have to forgo some frills in the launch process. Remember: You want to get your website online today, not a few months from now. Your website, if you launch it today starting from nothing, will probably look a lot like other people's websites at first.

And that's absolutely fine! Over time, you will be adding your own style and flavor to your website.

If it's a portfolio, a clean, blank site will make your work stand out even more.

If it's a blog, don't focus on how the site looks all around, but instead, focus on writing quality content that readers will engage with and share.

If you're starting an online store, focus on making quality products and show them off with your photos. Take photos of your products with your phone, put them on your site, then post them to an Instagram account linking each photo to the related product.

The mind blowing thing about all three of the scenarios above: You can start your website, create/update content and build an audience *all from your smartphone.* **A computer is no longer required to run an online business.**

Mind. Blown.

Eventually, you'll want to add to your ever growing website with things like a professional site design and logo, social media tools and analytics to track users and revenue. But, every journey starts with that first step. And if you set up too many tasks for yourself in the beginning, you're bound to never get there.

The Golden Rule for getting online within the day (and, if you're a designer, you've probably heard this one before): Less is more.

What You Will Need

Now, with all that being said, there are a few things you will need.

- **Basic Internet Skills**: If you know how to browse the web and have ever signed up for a free service before (Gmail, Facebook, etc), then you should be good.
- **Online Electronic Device**: This can be your home computer, smartphone or tablet. Something that can browse the web and allow you to type into websites should work fine.
- **A Modern Web Browser**: The architecture of the web changes daily, so your browser needs to be able to keep up. Recommended browsers: Chrome, Firefox, Safari. Check https://whatbrowser.org/ to check what browser you're using and see why you should always be using the latest version when browsing online.

- **Form of Payment**: Because the services listed in this guide, while cheap, are not free, you will need to have a way to pay for them to get yourself going. Typically, this means having a credit or debit card with a popular carrier (Visa, MasterCard, etc). Alternatively, some websites allow 3rd-party payment services, like PayPal, where you can directly link to a bank account instead of a card.
- **Patience**: With new challenges come new rewards, but the setup can be difficult even with a guide for those doing so for the first time. If you find yourself getting frustrated, walk away from the screen, take some deep breaths and relax before continuing. Patience will pay off.

What Type Of Site Do You Need?

This is where you plan your attack. This guide so far keeps touching on the same three types of examples: portfolio, blog and store. Your site might not fall into any of these categories; it might be a hybrid of two of these, or even be all three: Have a portfolio of work with blog posts describing the creative process for each specific piece and have it available for sale all in the same place. The sky's the limit!

As long as you know going in what your needs are, you can make a better decisions during the building stages as you create content and gather assets.

It's possible that you might not have any assets available to get on your site when you launch, but you can always add them in later. If this were a longer-term, planned out project, you'd have a web design ready to be coded, a professional logo made and all your site's imagery ready to go. But, again, if you wait to get all that together before launching, you might mentally hold yourself back and never get to where you want to be.

Add that stuff in later; let's get online today!

And it all starts with the right domain name.

.com .net .org

DOMAIN NAMES

Choosing a Domain Name

The first question you most like have is: What should I choose for my domain name?

Answer: Whatever fits your situation best.

There are many different types of TLDs (top-level domains) you could choose from, but for ease of memorization and association for your users/clients/ customers, you should stick to the popular three choices:

- **.com**: Used for commercially-based sites, and the most popular. If you're planning on selling yourself as a freelancer, plan on making money with your blog, or have an online store, definitely use a .com. Even if you're not, it doesn't hurt to own your-name.com just in case.
- **.net**: Used mainly by actual networks, but some individuals use this name as an alternative when their

.com is unavailable. Don't rule out .net!

- **.org**: Used by organizations. Perfect if you have a non-profit group; not so much if you plan on using the site to build a business.

Let's assume you want to go for a .com. What name should you choose?

Here are some recommendations, depending on your needs:

Portfolio Builder

Best bet, use "yourname.com". It'll match your business card, resume and, of course, your name. If you have a long or hard to spell name, a catchy nickname that you want to use professionally is also acceptable. For example, my default domain is cliffpro.com, even though cliffhuizenga. com works too. The former is far easier to remember, spell and pronounce.

Undecided on a specific name? You can always buy multiple domains. Your site will have to be set up under one domain by default, but secondary domains can easily forward to the primary.

Blogger

Are you writing a personal blog for yourself, or an add-on blog to your main portfolio site? Then follow the same route as the portfolio builder.

However, if your personal blog is targeted around a specific niche or you're devoting your entire blog to a particular industry, maybe a catchy name would better attract readers. Think of why the reader would come to your site: to read your thoughts, or to inform or help them with their interests? Are you the subject, or just the author behind your content? All things to consider when planning your blog.

Ecommerce / Storefront

Very simple answer: Your business name!

You business name is your brand and is more than likely the first name your customers will try to search for. So, why not make it easy for them to find you?

What if my Domain Choice is Taken?

If "yourname.com" is taken, you do have options:

Try a Variation of Your Name

If it's a personal name, try a nickname or a more common name used by others to address you. If your name is Katherine Myname, but everyone calls you Katie, use: katiemyname.com. You could also try adding in hyphens to the name: katie-myname.com. Or, target your profession in your domain directly: katiethedesigner.com.

Same applies for a blog name or business. If your business is "Carl's Cheese Cogs" and carlscheesecogs.com is taken, try variations removing or adding words that best describe your store. You could shorten the name: carlcheesecog. com Or, if you're located in a specific state, add the abbreviation in the address: carlscheesecogsct.com.

Use a Different TLD

If ownership of "yourname.anything" is important to you, you could see if a .net address is available for your business. Or you could look into other less popular TLD options that match your situation, such as .biz, .co, .ninja, etc. Who knows? Maybe you'll find one that will make you stand out from the crowd and give you a competitive edge!

Contact the Current Owner

Sometimes, people will own the domain for years without using them. Or, they can buy them out with the intention to never use it and to only turn a profit by selling it off— also known as "domain squatting". You could attempt to run a "whois" search with a domain provider to see their contact information. Whether it's a public email address or phone number for the owner directly, or if it's the domain registrar protecting their identity, there's usually contact info for you to reach out and ask about the ownership. Sometimes, the owner is willing to sell if it's worth their while and, while rare, might even let it go for cheap/free. No harm in asking!

Dispute Ownership with Trademarks

This one is a little extreme and not recommended. However, if you own a legitimate trademark issued from the USPTO (if you're from the United States) and can prove that their ownership of the domain infringes on your trademark, you may have a case to win the domain back.

If you even have the precognition of a thought about going down this road, find and discuss with a lawyer who specializes in trademark ownership to see if this is the best option for you. 99% of the time, this will not apply to you and you should consider the aforementioned options for domain name choosing.

Purchasing a Domain name

Domain name purchasing is probably the easiest part of the process to upgrade your online image. Just search for a name, see if it's available and, if it is, buy it. Done!

The hardest part of the domain hunt: finding a provider.

Easy Mode: Buy It Bundled With Hosting

Domains can be purchased separately, but more often than not, hosting providers will bundle domains with hosting packages. For example, sign up for a hosting plan and they might throw in the domain free for a year. If you have not purchased hosting and need to, hold off on getting a domain until you evaluate their offers.

Hard Mode: Buy It Separately

If you do end up getting a domain that doesn't come with hosting, you will need to follow instructions from the hosting provider to point your domain to them. But, it involves editing the DNS records for the domain name, specifically editing the A record to point to the IP address of the server. If you're going this route, make sure to shop around. Many providers give an excellent first year price for a domain name, then jack up the costs in subsequent years.

Here are some recommended domain providers:

- **Arvixe.com**: Not the easiest site to navigate, but their prices are great! Less than $10 per .com domain and if you own several domains, they'll give you a discount for each one.
- **Namecheap.com**: Also a great site for cheap domains with a more friendlier interface. Around $10 for a .com, Namecheap also offers hosting services. Plus, if you're looking to get an SSL Certificate (if you're running an online store), their prices are one of the cheapest in the business.

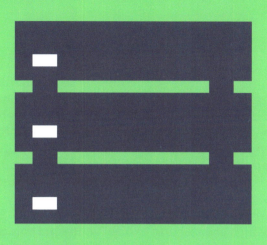

WEB HOSTING

Web Hosting Options

If a domain name address is the equivalent of a mailing address, then web hosting is the building located at the mailing address. Your web hosting will hold all the files required to run your website. And the starting point in obtaining hosting is choosing a hosting provider.

While you should be aware of which provider you choose and what reviews say about them, don't focus on searching for the right company first; focus on what kind of hosting you need, then find a hosting provider that can do so reliably and for a good price.

To do that, you'll need to understand what kinds of web hosting are available:

- **Shared Hosting (~$10/mo.):** This is the cheapest option available and, if you're making a quick portfolio site or starting a small blog, could be your best choice. Shared Hosting is where a hosting provider has you share your site(s) on the same server as many other customers. Because you're all sharing the same space, the cost of being there is less—much like roommates sharing an apartment. But, similarly, if one website—or yours—gets bogged down with traffic or gets hacked, everyone else on the server suffers. While it doesn't happen often, it could be an issue. If this is a concern, you might want to upgrade to a more premium solution.

- **WordPress (Managed) Hosting (~$30/mo.):** Some companies are starting to offer managed solutions for those running WordPress-based sites. By doing so, the hosting provider is in more control of what gets installed on their servers and can manage traffic and security far better. In return, you would also get better support from their staff which is very handy if you're not web-savvy enough to fix WordPress and server bugs yourself.
- **Virtual Private Server (VPS) (~$50-100/mo.):** If you know your way pretty well around a Linux server installation, know how to SSH in the back way, or know what a "cron job" is, you might benefit from a VPS. You get all the benefits of having a private server of your own, but in a virtual setting. You truly don't have a dedicated machine only for you, but the installation thinks it's dedicated, so it's more secure than a shared hosting plan. With it being digital, you gain more options for backups in case something goes wrong. If you're setting up an ecommerce store, but want to save a few bucks, it might be worth checking this option out. Just make sure you or someone you know can set things up or fix them if they break.
- **Dedicated Hosting (~$100+/mo.):** For the heavy-end, very server-savvy user. Unless the site you're launching will be huge right out of the gate, you won't need this. Maybe it can grow to this someday, but you're short on time and low on budget right now. So, stick with the above options.

Now that you have a rough idea on the differences between hosting plans, you can choose which one is best for you. More than likely, shared or managed WordPress hosting will be more than enough to get your site up and running today.

Hosting Recommendations

There are many companies out there to choose from, but it's hard to find out if a hosting provider supplies the best service for the price without actually signing up with them first. So, here's some suggestions to consider:

Quality Hosting: WP-Engine (wpengine.com)

WP Engine is a premiere hosting platform that specializes in premium WordPress hosting. While they are not the cheapest provider, the speed, reliability and security of their services is the biggest draw. Also, their knowledgeable and helpful support staff is of the quality you would expect. Whether you're super techy or a complete website noob, WP Engine will give you a professional, hassle-free experience for your website and growing business.

Budget, But Quality: Bluehost (bluehost.com)

If getting online quickly and on the cheap is important to you, then head on over to Bluehost. For about $6/mo., you can start to set up your site within minutes. Their shared hosting plan contains traditional control panel access with an option to easily install WordPress for you with a selection of themes that can be pre-installed—great if you need to get a portfolio online immediately!

MEET WORDPRESS

What is WordPress and Why Use It?

WordPress is a blogging-based platform that over the years has expanded to a full-blown content management system (CMS), handling websites such as, well, blogs, portfolios and stores, as well as so many other types of websites online.

But, why WordPress over another type of website? Here's a shortlist of reasons:

- **Usability**: WordPress is known for its easy-to-use interface and can be learned very quickly. If you can operate Microsoft Word, you can easily wrap your head around WordPress.
- **Versatility**: With their incredibly large number of plugins available with a single search and a click of a button, you can expand on WordPress to do just about

[3] 14 Surprising Statistics About WordPress Usage https://managewp. com/14-surprising-statistics-about-wordpress-usage

anything your heart desires. Add a few plugins and your WordPress site goes from being a blog to a store. All pretty easy stuff!

- **Security**: At the time of this writing, WordPress self-hosted websites make up 18.9% of all websites on the Internet.[3] As such, developers and companies have been improving how WordPress and its plugins keep your site and your site's visitors secure from hacks and other online dangers.

- **Themes**: Don't like how your website looks? Find a theme online and install it to your site! While you'll get better functionality and designs with a paid, professional theme, there are a ridiculous amount of free themes available for those on a budget and who want options.

You can already see why almost a fifth of the Internet uses WordPress: It makes getting their businesses online easier and it's more secure to maintain.

Installing WordPress (Very Quick, Introductory Version)

WordPress, while easy to use, can be a little bit of work to install. An entire book can be written on how to set up and run WordPress (and one might be in the works by this author, hint hint). But, for the sake of time to get you online faster, this book will only cover the basics to get you online and set up with a theme, minor plugins and content.

Initial Setup with WordPress Premium Hosting

The awesome thing about hosting services that specialize in dedicated WordPress hosting is that the install is either already done for you with your membership or is typically a few clicks away. Every site will differ, but there will probably be a section marked *Installs*, and an option of *Create/Add Install*. If it's your first WordPress site on your account, there will most likely be verbiage/graphical information on screen to guide you through setting up your site. If all else fails, contact their customer support or use a search engine to find blog/video tutorials on setting up for that provider.

Still, a managed, premium WordPress hosting option is the easiest way to run a WordPress site. You pay a little extra, but all the technical issues are taken care of by others.

Initial Setup with a Typical Website Hosting Provider

If you went with the option of a cheaper, shared hosting environment or a higher-end, but not WordPress-managed, self-hosted option, the process will take a few more steps.

If you're lucky, the hosting provider will have a control panel system similar to cPanel, which includes an awesome little tool called Fantastico. This blue smiley face will be able to install WordPress with just a few clicks and a few questions on setting up a user and password for the site—don't worry, Bluehost's got this.

However, if your host does not have a one-click WordPress install option, you can still get WordPress on your site. There's just more work involved. The following gives an overview—not a 100% follow-through method— of how to install WordPress on your hosting service by method of File Transfer Protocol (FTP):

- Download the latest WordPress install from http:// wordpress.org.
- Make sure your server has FTP access. You will also need to know the FTP address, username, and password, as well as if any other special requirements are necessary (port number, root directory, default directory, etc).
- Using your web host's control panel, create a new database for the install. You will most likely need to create a database username and password, then add that use to the newly created database. Take note of the database name, database username and password for later.
- Unpackage the WordPress .zip file you downloaded earlier.
- Connect to your site's FTP via an FTP client (FireFTP, Transmit, Filezilla, etc.).
- Upload the contents of the WordPress folder to the root directory of your site's FTP. Make sure you see all the files from the main WordPress folder in the FTP root directory—you should see folders like wp-content, wp-admin, and many .php files.
- Once the upload completes, open your web browser and go to your website's main domain ([your web

address].com).
- You should see a welcoming message from WordPress, ready to begin the install. If not, check to see if all the files were properly uploaded.
- When prompted, enter in your database name, database username and password. If all is working well, congrats on installing your own WordPress site!

Similar to the last section, if there's any portion that doesn't make sense, doesn't work, or throws errors, contact the customer support of your hosting or try to find a solution online from others with similar issues. (Honestly, you'd be surprised how many tutorial videos for WordPress installs are on YouTube.) WordPress is one of the easier web applications to install, but for someone who's never installed it before, it's quite intimidating. If getting your hands dirty in backend FTP uploads, PHP code edits and database building makes you uncomfortable, I would highly recommend either going with WP Engine or Bluehost for your hosting needs.

The Initial Setup Screen

If you've made it this far, then pop the confetti, because your website is officially online! W00t!

WordPress gives you a quick screen to edit the name of the blog/site and its description. For the description, type in a very short description, no longer than 150-160 characters. As you're building content for your site, when search engines find you, they will use this information when listing you in search results. There are more advanced controls that you can do for better visibility, but more on that in the Search Engine Optimization (SEO) section of this book.

When all that's entered in, you'll be taken to your brand new website's Dashboard.

The WordPress Dashboard

Welcome to the Dashboard! At first, you could get lost in the setup, but there are a few specific links in the left navigation for you to take notice:

- **Posts**: If you're writing a blog or generally writing updates on the website, this is where you do it.
- **Media**: All your images and media files will be uploaded here as your write posts and create pages. Get acquainted, especially if you're building a portfolio site.
- **Pages**: For non-chronological pages that don't get updated often, like an About or Contact page.
- **Comments**: If you're running a blog, this section will let you read, respond and filter comments on your posts. If you're not planning on using your site for blogging, make sure to disable comments sitewide, or leave them available for your blog but disabled on pages.
- **Appearance**: As you could guess, this changes how your site looks. The big sub-items in this section are:
  - **Themes**: The overall style and look of your site, dictated by an installed theme. WordPress comes with a number of their own by default, but you'll probably want something nicer (more on this later).
  - **Widgets**: If your theme supports them, you'll be able to add pre-made sections of info or apps to your site with very little code, like an archive list or a calendar.
  - **Menus**: Where you display links to the pages you've created on your site. Keeps people browsing around!
- **Plugins**: Added functionality to grow the power of your site and do things well beyond a traditional blog (more on this later too).
- **Users**: Shows what users are registered with the site. For the most part, the only user should be you, unless

you have a planned need for users, such as editors and guest posters.

- **Settings**: These options will control how the site's main info, how it will primarily function, how people will read your site and much more. As you add plugins, this section will likely grow (and, in some cases, so will the Tools section).

A Quick Note On Permalinks

By default, WordPress writes all the web addresses on your site as numerical page IDs ([mywebsite].com/?p=123) instead of human readable addresses ([mywebsite].com/page-name). To fix this, go to *Settings > Permalinks*, and change the Common Settings from *Default* to any of the other options that best suits your needs. If you're primarily writing a blog, the *Day and Name* or *Month and Name* options are nice for dated archives. Otherwise, if this is more of a full website that may or may not *include* a blog, the *Post Name* setting will give you clean page names.

Themes

If there is one section to this entire guide that will suck most of your time away, it's searching for the right WordPress theme. Considering the high install base of WordPress across the web, thousands—if not millions—of WordPress themes have been created. Looking for the one that best fits your needs to start off can waste a lot of time, but is well worth it if you find one that fits best for you.

The question in your mind though: *Where do I start to look for themes if there are so many to choose from?*

The problem here is that it's tough to judge how a theme will work on your site until you have it installed. Also, while many themes are free, some websites can be shady with including themes that have malware or other deceptive practices in the code. Yikes! So, how does one get around these issues of quality control?

First things first: **Do not** search for "free WordPress themes" in a search engine. You will fall down a deep rabbit hole of malicious download links and dead ends.

And the sad truth is, sometimes you get what you pay for; Free themes may be hit or miss and sometimes you need to decide when it's worth it to purchase a theme that will work best.

Recommended places to get quality themes:

- **Free themes within WordPress**: In your WordPress Dashboard, go to *Appearance > Themes*, click on the *Add New* button, and browse through the Featured and Popular categories of free themes ready to install with a few clicks.

- Search reputable websites for recommendations on current themes and new themes as they're released (see Additional WordPress Resources for more).
- **Themeforest by Envato Market (themeforest.net)**: One of the biggest collections of designer themes available. All themes have reviews from customers and live demos to see how the theme will actively look online. (Avg. theme price ~ $40)
- **WooThemes (woothemes.com)**: A nice, focused collection of premium themes. Highly recommended if you are going to run an online store with your WordPress site, as they are the creators of WooCommerce, one of the best shopping plugins for WordPress. (Avg. theme price ~$40-80+, includes some free themes)
- **Genesis Framework (studiopress.com)**: Frameworks can help with getting a functional baseline in website operations and optimization, which also can be customized with themes specifically designed and built for those frameworks. Genesis, while a little pricier than one-off themes from Themeforest, are some of the highest quality themes you can find, and they offer a bundle discount if you buy all their themes in one shot. (~$60 for the framework; ~$80 for the framework with a single theme; ~$400 for the framework and all 40+ themes)
- **Qards (designmodo.com/qards)**: This one is really a plugin and not a theme, but if you're still having issues finding a good theme that's easy to customize and if you don't mind dropping ~$99 to make it easy on you, Qards gives you an entire drag-and-drop site building experience. Check out their demo video on their site and try to not be impressed.

So much more can be said for theme hunting, but hopefully this will get you started in the right direction. Try to limit yourself on how much time you search. As your site grows, your theme needs will change.

Remember: you want to get your website going today, not next week.

And that might even mean using a default, pre-installed WordPress theme to get yourself started.

But, the true power of WordPress is in its flexibility that comes from plugins.

Plugins

WordPress does a great job with running a nice, easy-to-use site out of the box. But, if you want to beef up your standing on the internet, you'll want to utilize the power of plugins.

Plugins can add a whole new set of functionality to your site, allowing for greater usability, automation, security and housekeeping. There's a plugin for just about anything you can think of!

Of course, of all the plugins out there, you'll find decent ones and you'll find excellent ones. Depending on your kind of site, here are a few plugin recommendations to look into while starting off:

- **AdSanity**: Planning on placing ads on your site/blog? AdSanity gives you the ability to organize and schedule which ads get placed into rotation. Great if you have paying advertisers or a high-traffic site to pair with Google Adsense.
- **Akismet**: A free plugin designed to filter out comment spam (when fake, robotic comments get posted on your site instead of real people). Definitely take advantage of this one.
- **Contact Form 7**: Of course, if you're looking for a free form builder, Contact Form 7 will do an amazing job with your forms as well! You'll just need to learn how to use WordPress' "shortcode" functionality to activate them.
- **Disqus**: This free plugin adds a 3rd-party commenting service that allows people to represent themselves from their social media profiles when commenting and also allows for comments to be backed up and archived online. Excellent features too!
- **Google Analytics Dashboard**: If you create a Google Analytics account, you'll be able to integrate it with this free dashboard plugin to see how your site's

traffic and performance is right on your WordPress Dashboard screen.

- **Gravity Forms**: Need forms on your site? Gravity Forms gives you the easiest customization for the money. If you like the idea of drag-and-drop-to-build forms, this is one you'll want.
- **Jetpack by WordPress**: A whole truckload of free tools from WordPress on tracking visitors, post-sharing options, publicizing, and more!
- **MailChimp**: If you start to build an audience, you'll want to capture their attention for future marketing materials. Be ready for them with a mailing list for them to sign up for!
- **WooCommerce**: Plan on running an online store? WooCommerce is your solution. The free plugin transforms your website into a whole storefront, ready for you to sell whatever you want. Add-ons for WooCommerce can be pricey, but you can still get away with doing a lot for free or cheap.
- **WordPress SEO by Yoast**: If you plan on blogging or selling products, your site's going to need to tell search engines the right information for your potential visitors/customers. This free plugin will give you the tools needed to optimize your posts/pages presence to search engines. Definitely learn more about SEO before using, but don't write off this one.
- **WP Mail SMTP**: Some hosting providers are excellent with WordPress sending out emails for maintenance and alerts; and some hosting providers are not. If you have SMTP credentials for your Gmail or other email account, you can add them in here and have WordPress email you when it needs to if your hosting fails to do so.
- **W3 Total Cache**: Blog posts will update all the time, but what about static pages? If they aren't changing often, use this plugin to save parts of your site locally on the user's computer. This eliminates waiting for the site to load, making it faster and more appealing to readers and search engines.

Additional WordPress Resources

For those looking to learn more about WordPress' inner workings, both to simply use the front-end and those looking to get their hands dirty with code, take a look at these resources:

- **WPBeginner (wpbeginner.com)**: Great articles about learning WordPress and doing simple codes for common functionality requests.
- **WP Tuts+ (code.tutsplus.com/categories/ wordpress)**: Plan on going a little more in with learning? The tutorials featured here are worth taking a browse through.
- **Treehouse (teamtreehouse.com)**: Highly recommended education service with video tutorials to help you build, grow and market your own WordPress site, as well as learn HTML/CSS, other coding languages, and even help you build your business. I'm a proud member myself!
- **WordPress Codex (codex.wordpress.org)**: The source for really going deep in the WordPress code. Learn all the functions and be able to work with them to create anything you desire.

ALTERNATIVES TO SELF-HOSTED WORDPRESS

After all that, you may still be thinking of trying something else other than good old WP. That's fine! Whatever tool gets the job done is the best one.

There are other CMS options for self-hosted websites, but if WordPress is not appealing to you, it might be because it could be a little much for someone completely new to owning their own website. If this is the case, it could be recommended to not purchase self-hosted web space and, instead, go with a web service that makes creating your website even easier and allows you to attach your domain name for viewing. You may not be able to greatly expand on your site by going with one of the following options, but hey, you'll be online today as well, so they work!

Possible Options For You:

- **For the portfolio builder**: Behance by Adobe (creative.adobe.com/products/pro-site) has a ProSite feature that can turn your work into an awesome looking portfolio for people to browse and "Appreciate" with Like-style buttons. You can give the option of letting people contact you about your work and link to external sites (like your resume). It's currently included with a Creative Cloud subscription which can be a little pricey, but includes all of Adobe's software. So, if you're in the market for Photoshop anyway, why not get a free portfolio site to go with it?
- **For the store owner**: Shopify (shopify.com) has one of the easiest setups for starting your online store. While it may not be as flexible as WooCommerce in WordPress, it will definitely get your store online today with the most minimal work possible. With several payment gateways, reporting, inventory and built-in themes, you can have a unique store ready to go when you want it. Plans start around $29/mo.
- **For the all-in-one(der)**: Squarespace (squarespace.com) aims to be the everything you need to get online as fast as humanly possible. Customization options from the design of the site to stock photography options and even logo templates to create your own brand identity, they'll make sure you make a good first impression online. Plans starting at $8/mo.

The only downside to using one of these services is how you could be paying too much to get the same, or better, functionality from a self-hosted WordPress website. Also, you might find you'll outgrow your website (if all goes well, of course) and will need something more robust that your non-self-hosted site cannot offer, or can but will cost much more. That is the trade-off though: your site will do whatever you want it to for little effort, but you're going to pay for that convenience.

Then again, if you're more about convenience in getting your site online today and don't mind spending the few extra bucks, why not? Paying more to get your presence online faster is better than not launching at all.

With that being said, decide what your next move is and get your site online!

POST-PURCHASE AND LAUNCH

If you made it this far, guess what? You just launched a website! Throw more confetti!!

Obviously, this is only the beginning as there's still plenty to do for the long-term. Things to consider either now or down the road:

Email Integration

Since you own a .com address and a website, how cool would it be to have your email address match? Definitely consider making a custom email address to go with your domain (your-name@your-website.com). Google Apps gives the best options for the price (~$5/mo.) and gives your email the power of Google's Gmail, but with your personalized email address instead! Google will guide you through the setup and domain verification process, but it's not too difficult to install.

Search Engine Optimization (SEO)

The Holy Grail of the Internet! SEO is the combination of methods and tools used to change content on a website in order to rank higher in search engines for a specific set of topics. Basically, if you're asking, "How to I get to number 1 on Google for searching X," then SEO is what you're after.

However, learning SEO does not happen overnight and many people have high-paying careers in helping people and companies with better SEO for their sites to bring in more customers. There are many differing opinions on what to do to optimize a page of content on the web. But, if you're serious about growing your online business, it would be wise to look into learning about SEO and maybe even hiring a professional to let you know what you can do to bring in more people and more revenue.

Mailing List

If you're planning on blogging or have an online store, you need to keep connected to your readers and customers. A great way to engage them is by having an email list for them to sign up to. Even a simple weekly update is enough to keep them coming back. If you're selling products, use the list to advertise your latest products or special deals. If you're a blogger, share an excerpt from your latest post and then link back to the full article online (and take advantage of affiliate marketing/ads for added revenue).

There are different email list providers you can choose from, many of which have excellent marketing capabilities. However, if you're just starting off, go with a service like MailChimp (mailchimp.com). As their service is free up to 2,000 subscribers, you have plenty of time to build an audience before it starts to cost you anything.

Social Media

Along with email, connecting with your audience significantly increases engagement, as they can gain a deeper connection to you through social media interaction. So, definitely make dedicated social media profiles to cover your professional image and/or your business. Big ones to hit:

- **Twitter (twitter.com)**: great for quick updates and immediate feedback to/from your audience. "Tweets" are limited to 140 characters, but allow for less clutter than other social media sites while still allowing for multimedia such as images, audio and video to be included.
- **Facebook (facebook.com)**: The big kahuna. With almost 1.4 billion active users by the end of 2014, Facebook's audience cannot be denied. At the very least, create a Facebook page for your online business to push content to.
- **Instagram (instagram.com / mobile app)**: Is your site image heavy? Perfect! Use Instagram to target an audience of photo lovers and drive more people back with visuals and hooks on what you're promoting.
- **Pinterest (pinterest.com)**: A great way to share images from your website as well as share images from other websites into collections for people to browse and enjoy. When people share your pictures, they create links back to your website, which generates more traffic for you!
- **YouTube (youtube.com)**: Creating videos can be time consuming if you want them to look super professional, but with our phones having better quality cameras, anyone can make a decent-looking video to share—and the content of the video is king. Create valuable and entertaining videos, start up a channel on YouTube and build subscribers.
- **Vine (vine.com / mobile app)**: Similar to YouTube, but limited to 6 second bursts. While it sounds like it would be impossible to generate traffic from here, you

could definitely find creative ways to utilize Vine in your marketing efforts.

All these avenues are great ways to build your audience. Find ways to make them connect to other social accounts or back to the main site. Maybe use them to announce contests or promotions. Or, just make something entertaining to share in the hopes it goes viral (NOTE: do not *try* to make a viral video; people can tell when you're trying too hard and it doesn't work). Use these social accounts to build a larger audience to achieve the goals of your business.

Also, even if you see a large amount of activity with one social media account, you should never put all your eggs in one basket and only focus on that one. If one is going strong, definitely work harder with that one to keep momentum up. But, don't disregard others just because they haven't hit their stride. Different content shares differently on different social networks, because they're all... well, different.

Cast the widest nets you can, cover as many areas you can, and check back often to see if you caught anything. This is another reason why email list marketing is so important, because people have come to you *directly* wanting to know more about what you have to say and sell. use social media to drive them to your mailing list or, better yet, a landing page on your site that gets people to sign up for your list or buy your product or... whatever it is you want them to do.

But, whatever interactions you promote on any medium, remember that your main site should be the final destination for all of these people. Have unique content on your social media accounts, but make sure the final call to action for each post leads them back to your door. Otherwise, they'll stop at the social media pages with a few "Likes" and maybe a share without going to your site at all.

"If you build it, they will come" works, but only if they know where "it" is. Show them.

Google+

Google tried their hand at social media by introducing Google+ and while their user interaction is very high (make a post and expect people to reply), the audience using the service is quite minimal. So, the question is, "Should Google+ be used to promote my business site?"

Surprisingly, an argument can be made for creating a Google+ Page for your business. Main reason is because it creates a listing online for the business. It gives you another avenue for pushing content to and with Google being one of the best search engines online, your content has a better chance of showing up in search results (on their system) by using them.

Who knows? Maybe your content takes off on Google+ stronger than other social media sites. Listen to your audience and pay attention to their behaviors. Look at what's happening in the short term and then try to see down the road for what could be.

Plus, if you're "on the map," you'll need a Google+ Page set up to be found.

Google Maps

If you have a physical location, this is an absolute must. People will be able to connect better to your online business if they know you also exist in the physical world.

Now, I'm not going to lie: setting up your location for Google Maps can be a process, now that Google's gone all + on everything. The issue is that, for Google to add your location to Maps, they need to verify you actually are at the location you specify. To keep the process secure they

do two steps:
1. Google creates a whole new + Page just for business verification; and
2. Google sends a physical postcard to the address you specify, which includes a verification code you'll need to finish setup. This part can take 1-2 weeks.

If you never set up a Google+ Page for your business, Google's kind of helping you out by making one for you. However, if you already made a page previously, this could be misunderstood as being forced to have two pages. Thankfully, Google's got instructions on how to either set up a local page from scratch or migrate the location verification to your currently-made Google+ Page:

• If you've never set up a Google+ Page for your business, follow these instructions to get your local business listed: https://support.google.com/business/answer/2911778
• If you already created a Google+ Page for your business, go with these instructions instead: https://support.google.com/business/answer/6010825

Revenue Generation

This part is mainly for the bloggers out there, but could really apply to any kind of site. Many bloggers run full-time businesses just from online blogging, offering their advice and services in the form of free blog posts you can subscribe to. But, if they're just giving their content away, how are they making money?

There's a few tactics they're using (and you can too):

• **Email Lists**: There it is again! Yup, email lists are still an excellent way to promote website content, products you create or services being offered by you or others paying you to do so. Don't be afraid to look into promotional offers by others.

- **Paid Posts**: Companies are willing to pay to have you blog about their products or services on your blog. If your website is relevant to their products, definitely consider doing so down the road. Also, if your site gets a large number of readers daily, you can command a higher rate for doing paid posts.
- **Paid Advertisements**: There's also the option of showing a company's ad on your site for a predetermined amount of time. Use a plugin like AdSanity (if your site is WordPress-based) to schedule the rotation of their and others' ads. And speaking of ads...
- **Google AdSense (google.com/adsense/start)**: Google has their own ad program to bring you extra revenue. Just generate an ad block in their system, then add it to your site. Done! Don't overdo it, or they penalize you. Only put up to 3 Google Ads on your site. It will make your site look cleaner and open room for other companies to directly connect with you for ad revenue.
- **Affiliate Marketing Partners**: Here's where one of the big money makers comes in: There are full websites dedicated to offering ads and even specialty product links to write about and connect to. Review a product or store, link to their site using a generated affiliate link, and get paid if the reader buys something from the advertiser's site. You can join groups such as CJ Affiliate by Conversant (cj.com) or LinkShare (marketing.rakuten.com/affiliate-marketing) to get all the tools you need to make it happen. But, if you ask anyone what the king of affiliate payouts is, they would probably all choose...
- **Amazon Associates Program (affiliate-program. amazon.com)**: Good old Amazon! Not only do they have the largest catalogue of products available online, they're also one of the highest paying affiliate programs you'll find online. Do a review, link to the product and, whether they buy it or not, if your reader

buys anything on Amazon, you might get commission on the sale. How awesome is that?

A Note on Affiliate Marketing and Paid Promotions

Due to FTC guidelines, you are required to disclose when you are using affiliate marketing and being paid (or being given something of monetary value) for your review/ product. This prevents the reader from being misled in thinking you're giving an honest review if you are truly only doing so for the money.

However, if you are honestly endorsing a product that you believe in and you got paid for doing so, there's absolutely no shame in letting your readers know. It builds trust with them because you're being honest and, let's be serious, you shouldn't have to hide that you're making money from your passions. If people don't agree with it, they don't need to take in your work.

For example, this book you're reading right now includes links to affiliates that I believe will give you the best bang for your buck. The benefits are two-fold: I offer to you services that will help you get your website off the ground and your business idea out of your head and into the wild; if you decide to use one of my mentioned services using the links I supply in this book, your paid participation in those services gives me a little something extra back.

And, if you find those services to be helpful, you too can set up affiliate accounts and earn commissions for yourself through your readers and connections. Comes back full circle!

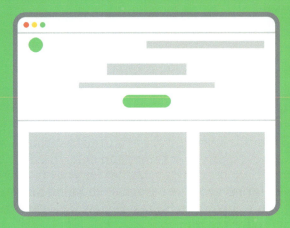

THE REST IS UP TO YOU

By this point, you should have the following done:

- Purchased a domain name & web hosting
- Obtained a dedicated email address
- If you chose to go WordPress, you also should have:
    - Set up your WordPress site & learned the interface
    - Made a few pages and possibly blog posts
    - Uploaded imagery/content
    - Looked into themes and plugins
- Thought about where you'd like to go from here

As I mentioned before, there's so much more to do and so much room for you to grow. But sometimes, the hardest part of the journey is that first step. And if you made it this far, you've not only made the first steps, but you've walked the first mile.

And if I had to guess, things weren't exactly as smooth as you would have hoped them to be. This is normal! You'll have struggles. But, the ones who succeed are the ones who overcome those struggles. Look up information online, read tutorials and, most importantly, ask for help when you need it.

To know where you're headed from here, that's all up to you.

To (nerdly) quote Morpheus from the movie, The Matrix, "I'm trying to free your mind, Neo. But I can only show you the door. You're the one that has to walk through it."

If your site is online, then you walked through the door. If you've thought about what you want to do, you've got an idea of the road in front of you.

Now, it's time to run. Go!

THE END OF THIS BOOK
ONE MORE FINAL:
I thank you.

ONE MORE FINAL:
I THANK YOU

As you run your new path and business, I want to once again thank you for your support by purchasing this book. This is the first ebook I've ever released and I truly hope it helps you achieve your goals and dreams.

I started writing this book on the side after people would ask me for the same website help over and over; teaching them how to start up a site, get a domain, setup a blog, maintain WordPress, etc. And in most cases, the individuals didn't have the technical knowledge to get things off the ground.

But they all shared the same thing: passion.

They all had a passion for their craft, their ideas and their self worth.

So, I wanted to write this book for them. And, surprisingly, it almost didn't happen.

I made my own excuses. "I don't have time." "Who would read it?" I was my own personal barrier.

Then, finally, one day I snapped. I was tired of making excuses and holding myself back from doing something. If I'm able to help start a business with my wife selling confetti, I most definitely could write a book on something I do practically every day.

I started to blog about the writing process, set myself a time limit for writing, revising, organizing, designing and launching the book.

You're seeing the results of that process. You've helped invest in my passion.

Now, go invest in yours.

I wish to express my deepest thanks for your time and, in return, if you need any advice on any topic covered in the book, you're more than welcome to send me a message. I'd be thrilled to see your response to my work.

Take care and keep being awesome!

Cliff Huizenga
Email: me@cliffpro.com
Website: cliffpro.com
Twitter: @Cliffpro

LEGAL

The electronic version of this book contains affiliate links, identifiable in green styling. By signing up for the services offered by these affiliate links, the author will gain monetary compensation for the referral (and he sends his thanks to you for your continued awesomeness).

The WordPress name is owned by the WordPress Foundation. All other company names mentioned in this book are owned by their respective owners.

COLOPHON

Headlines use Bebas Neue font by Svetoslav Simov / Fontfabric™. Body copy uses Arvo font by Anton Koovit.

ABOUT THE AUTHOR

Cliff Huizenga is a web designer, front-end developer and avid gamer. He has been professionally working in web design and development for the past decade, having been with different agencies and working with clients of all sizes. He prefers minimal, responsive web design.

Cliff is also the Co-Owner and Director of Digital Awesomeness of The Confetti Bar (theconfettibar.com). Along with his wonderful wife, Jessica, he helps spread happiness and celebration to the world with custom confetti mixes and shapes designed for any occasion.

When not helping clients with their website and marketing needs, Cliff's working on his ~~30th~~ 31st logo redesign, updating his website (cliffpro.com), rambling on his Twitter (@Cliffpro) or playing either retro video games or modern games online with an occasional live stream. If you want to chat with him, send Cliff an email at: me@cliffpro.com.

www.ingramcontent.com/pod-product-compliance
Lightning Source LLC
Chambersburg PA
CBHW041150050326
40689CB00004B/717